BE

ANTIRACIST

A JOURNAL FOR AWARENESS, REFLECTION & ACTION

IBRAM X. KENDI

ONE WORLD

New York

Introduction

From the start, I feared sharing my racial journey with the public. I did not want the world to see the most shameful and foolish and embarrassing moments of my racial life. I did not want to write *How to Be an Antiracist*, which came out on my birthday in 2019. I did not want *this* birthday present. I did not want the public to read a journal of my innermost racial thoughts. I wanted to keep these thoughts private. I wanted a journal for me, and me alone, that I might possibly share with others when I was ready. And I wasn't ready.

Love dissolved my fears. Love for humanity, love for myself, and love for you. I wanted to overcome my own internalized racism. I want humans everywhere to overcome theirs. I want to publicly encourage and guide journaling on race. Therefore, this journal is for you and you alone. But I hope it becomes something you can share with others when you are ready.

The heartbeat of racism is denial. Each day, we are discouraged from honestly reflecting on our ideas and actions toward particular racial groups. Each day, we are encouraged to deny whenever we are being racist. What fuels racism is refusing to self-reflect, defining *racist* in a way that exonerates us. It is constantly declaring that we are *not racist*. All the time. No matter what we say or do.

The heartbeat of antiracism is confession. It is self-reflection. It is realizing that there is no such thing as *not racist*, no such thing as race neutrality. It is realizing that all ideas and policies are either racist or antiracist; all people are *being* racist or antiracist. No one *becomes* a racist or an antiracist. These are not fixed categories. We can be racist one moment and antiracist the next. What we say about the races, what we do about inequity determines what—not who—we are in each moment.

But to determine what we are we must define what *racist* and *antiracist* are in a clear and consistent way. After defining these terms, we can apply them to ourselves, to the ideas we express, to the policies we support and to our action and inaction when staring in the face of inequity and injustice. After applying those terms to ourselves, we can constantly declare to ourselves and to the world the moments we are being racist.

My book, *How to Be an Antiracist*, is my confessional. It is my antiracist journal. I defined terms and reflected on my racial views of power, biology, ethnicity, the body, culture, behavior, Whiteness, Blackness, class, space, gender, and sexual orientation. I reflected on my racism, on how I am surviving racism, on how our society can survive racism.

This is your antiracist journal. It can be your confessional. I want you to be painfully honest with yourself as you document your racial journey. Walk with me and others; guide yourself and others. Let this journal prompt constructive conversations with colleagues, friends, and loved ones. Complete journal entries with youngsters. Complete this journal in a weekend or complete an entry per day or an entry per week as a regular antiracist practice. Because, like everything else, being antiracist is about practice—regular practice—and reflecting on our practice.

We must continuously reflect on ourselves so we can reflect on our society. We must continuously strive to be antiracist so we can build an antiracist society. An antiracist society not governed by fear and hate and cynicism, but one of equity and justice and truth. An antiracist society governed by curiosity and love and hope, honoring humanity in all its fullness.

This is your antiracist journal. It can be your confessional. I want you to be painfully honest with yourself as you document your racial journey.

IN FREEDOM,

APRIL 2020

"What's the problem with being 'not racist'? It is a claim that signifies neutrality: 'I am not a racist, but neither am

I aggressively against racism.' But there is no neutrality in the racism struggle. The opposite of 'racist' isn't 'not racist.' It is 'antiracist.'"

Have you ever described yourself as "not racist"? What does *not racist* mean to you? Why do you think so many people are invested in believing that they are "not racist"?

Why are so many people invested in believing there is race neutrality? What is the relationship between believing in race neutrality and identifying as "not racist"?

DATE   /   /

"'They think it's okay not to think!' I charged, raising the classic racist idea that Black youth don't value education as much as their non-Black counterparts. No one seemed to care that this well-traveled idea had flown on anecdotes but had never been grounded in proof. Still, the crowd encouraged me with their applause. I kept shooting out unproven and disproven racist ideas about all the things wrong with Black youth—ironically, on the day when all the things right about Black youth were on display."

It was hard to begin *How to Be an Antiracist* with a confession of the most racist moment of my life, a speech I gave as a high school senior for a Martin Luther King Jr. oratorical competition. But I figured the confessions would get easier. And they did.

Describe the most racist moment of your life.

_____

_____

_____

_____

_____

_____

_____

_____

_____

_____

_____

_____

_____

_____

_____

_____

Why do you consider this the most racist moment of your life? What should you have done or said differently?

I should have pointed out that racism was the problem in my MLK speech, not Black youth.

"Racist ideas make people of color think less of themselves, which makes them more vulnerable to racist ideas. Racist ideas make White people think more of themselves, which further attracts them to racist ideas."

Racist ideas prevent us from being grounded, keeping our views of ourselves too high or too low as a result of racist ideas about the superiority of our own racial group.

Chronicle a time when you thought too highly of yourself as a result of racist ideas about your own racial group.

Reflect on a time when you thought too little of yourself as a result of racist ideas about the inferiority of your own racial group.

Why is abolishing the "not racist" neutrality and identity so vital to freeing us to be antiracist?

To be antiracist is to be grounded in your humanity.

Name five issues, people, or memories that may have prevented you from being grounded in your own equal humanity.

1

2

3

4

5

"**Definitions** anchor us in principles. This is not a light point: If we don't do the basic work of defining the kind of people we want to be in language that is stable and consistent, we can't work toward stable, consistent goals. Some of my most consequential steps toward being an antiracist have been the moments when I arrived at basic definitions."

Define the following terms

Race

Racist idea

Antiracist idea

Racial inequity

Racial equity

Racist policy

Antiracist policy

Racism

Antiracism

Racist (person)

Antiracist (person)

My Definitions

Race

A power construct of blended human difference that lives socially.

Racist idea

Any idea suggesting that one racial group is inferior or superior to another racial group in any way.

Antiracist idea

Any idea suggesting that the racial groups are equal in all their apparent differences.

Racial inequity

When two or more racial groups are not standing on a relatively equal footing.

Racial equity

When two or more racial groups are standing on a relatively equal footing.

Racist policy

Any measure that produces or sustains racial inequity among racial groups.

Antiracist policy

Any measure that produces or sustains racial equity among racial groups.

Racism

A powerful collection of racist policies that leads to racial inequity and is substantiated by racist ideas.

Antiracism

A powerful collection of antiracist policies that leads to racial equity and is substantiated by antiracist ideas.

Racist (person)

One who is supporting a racist policy through their actions or inaction or expressing a racist idea.

Antiracist (person)

One who is supporting an antiracist policy through their actions or expressing an antiracist idea.

List and describe five major experiences
that have most influenced how you relate to
racial issues.

1

2

3

4

5

Who do you most look up to on race? What
are their views? Why have you been drawn
to those views? Would you categorize those
views as antiracist or racist, based on the
definitions on page 19?

Who or what scares you the most when you think about race? Why?

How would you characterize the current state
of racial affairs in your community?

List at least three additional words or phrases that make it easier for people to talk about or around the R-word: racism.

DATE   /   /

1

2

3

"'Microaggression' became part of a whole vocabulary of old and new words— like 'cultural wars' and 'stereotype' and 'implicit bias' and 'economic anxiety' and 'tribalism'—that made it easier to talk about or around the R-word."

Have you ever been hesitant to use the
R-word? Why?

_____

_____

_____

_____

_____

_____

_____

_____

_____

_____

_____

_____

_____

_____

_____

_____

_____

_____

_____

_____

_____

_____

Why is it necessary for antiracists to use the R-word?

"At seven years old, I began to feel the encroaching fog of racism overtaking my dark body. It felt big, bigger than me, bigger than my parents or anything in my world, and threatening. What a powerful construction race is—powerful enough to consume us. And it comes for us early."

When did race come for you? Describe in
detail your earliest memory when you saw the
world through a racial lens.

DATE   /   /

_____

_____

_____

_____

_____

_____

_____

_____

_____

_____

_____

_____

_____

_____

_____

_____

_____

_____

_____

Race probably came for you and shaped your life before this moment.

What forces could have been shaping your racial life before you realized it?

_____

_____

_____

_____

_____

_____

_____

_____

_____

_____

_____

_____

_____

_____

_____

_____

_____

_____

Describe the first time you challenged (or thought about challenging) racism.

DATE   /   /

Name a time when you regret not challenging racism. What could you have done differently?

_____

_____

_____

_____

_____

_____

_____

_____

_____

_____

_____

_____

_____

_____

_____

_____

_____

_____

_____

"Race is a mirage but one that we do well to see, while never forgetting it is a mirage, never forgetting that it's the powerful light of racist power that makes the mirage."

How is race a mirage?

In what ways should we look at race?

In what ways should we not look at race?

"If we stop using racial categories, then we will not be able to identify racial inequity. If we cannot identify racial inequity, then we will not be able to identify racist policies. If we cannot identify racist policies, then we cannot challenge racist policies. If we cannot challenge racist policies, then racist power's final solution will be achieved: a world of inequity none of us can see, let alone resist."

Are the people calling for "race-neutral" policies also calling for the elimination of racial inequities? Why or why not?

Why is calling for presumably "race-neutral" policies the final racist solution?

Why is it dangerous to call a society where racial inequities persist "post-racial"?

Define and describe a White ethnostate. How would it be any different from society right now?

How could a "race-neutral" state be more threatening than the movement for a White ethnostate?

Describe an antiracist state. How would it be any different from society right now?

"Some of us are restrained by fear of what could happen to us if we resist. In our naïveté, we are less fearful of what could happen to us—or is already happening to us—if we don't resist."

What does *resistance* mean to you?

What happens to us if we don't resist? What happens when we do?

Consider an example of this cause and effect from the past and an example from the present. Explain these two examples.

Past

Present

"[A] racist power creates racist policies out of raw self-interest; the racist policies necessitate racist ideas to justify them—[this cause and effect] lingers over the life of racism."

"Seventy-one percent of White families lived in owner-occupied homes in 2014, compared to 45 percent of Latinx families and 41 percent of Black families."

Consider the following racial inequity in the United States, as revealed by the Stanford Center on Poverty and Inequality in 2017.

What racist ideas normalize inequities like this?

_____
_____
_____
_____
_____
_____
_____
_____
_____
_____
_____
_____
_____
_____
_____
_____
_____

What antiracist ideas could make these inequities seem abnormal? What antiracist policies could reduce or eliminate these inequities?

"Americans have long been trained to see the deficiencies of people rather than policy. It's a pretty easy mistake to make: People are in our faces. Policies are distant. We are particularly poor at seeing the policies lurking behind the struggles of people."

Think about a person of color you saw struggling recently. What policies could be lurking behind that person's struggles? What racist ideas could be preventing people from recognizing those policies?

_____

_____

_____

_____

_____

_____

_____

_____

_____

_____

_____

_____

_____

_____

_____

_____

_____

_____

_____

DATE / /

"A racist idea is any idea that suggests one racial group is inferior or superior to another racial group in any way. Racist ideas argue that it is the inferiorities and superiorities of racial groups that explain racial inequities in society."

List something you think is wrong with Black people, or any particular group of Black people.

FOR EXAMPLE: *I used to think Black youth didn't value education.*

List something you think is wrong with Asian people, or any particular group of Asian people.

FOR EXAMPLE: *I used to believe Asian men were compliant.*

List something you think is wrong with Middle Eastern people, or any particular group of Middle Eastern people.

FOR EXAMPLE: *I used to imagine Middle Eastern women as submissive.*

List something you think is wrong with Indigenous people, or any particular group of Indigenous people.

FOR EXAMPLE: *I used to think Indigenous people were weak.*

List something you think is wrong with White people, or any particular group of White people.

FOR EXAMPLE: *I used to think White people were evil.*

List something you think is wrong with Latinx people, or any particular group of Latinx people.

FOR EXAMPLE: *I used to think Latinx immigrants were taking Black jobs.*

"My parents—even from within their racial consciousness—were susceptible to the racist idea that it was laziness that kept Black people down, so they paid more attention to chastising Black people than to Reagan's policies, which were chopping the ladder they climbed up and then punishing people for falling."

Name three opportunities that impoverished Blacks do not normally receive that can keep them from climbing the socioeconomic ladder.

1

2

3

DATE   /   /

Think about your life as a ladder. Specify and reflect on three opportunities you have received that were crucial to your climb.

1

2

3

What is your relationship to your racial identity? Do you feel connected to or separated from your racial identity? Why?

"Assimilationists can position any racial group as the superior standard that another racial group should be measuring themselves against, the benchmark they should be trying to reach. Assimilationists typically position White people as the superior standard."

I standardized White people for much of my life without knowing it.

DATE   /   /

Make a list of 10 phrases or sayings used in everyday conversation or in the media that reinforce Whiteness or White people as the superior standard.

FOR EXAMPLE: *Identifying European history as world history.*

1

2

3

4

5

6

7

8

9

10

If we should not be standardizing the ways and likeness of a racial group, then how should an antiracist view cultural and bodily differences among the racial groups?

It is widely believed that (1) human behavior is derived from human genes and (2) different races have different genes. The first idea has never been proven, and the second idea has been roundly disproven.

DATE   /   /

Why is the first idea as dangerous in fomenting racism as the second idea?

"Biological racism rests on two ideas: that the races are meaningfully different in their biology and that these differences create a hierarchy of value. . . . To be antiracist is to recognize the reality of biological equality, that skin color is as meaningless to our underlying humanity as the clothes we wear over that skin."

List three *biological* qualities you think, or once thought, Indigenous people had. What about Black people? White people?

DATE _____ / _____ / _____

FOR EXAMPLE: *I used to think that Indigenous people were spiritual by nature, Black people were talented dancers by nature, and White people were individualistic by nature.*

1

2

3

Why is it so important to see different skin colors as meaningless to our underlying humanity and as meaningful in their beautiful diversity?

Some Americans think the solution to color hierarchies is not to see color at all, or for all humans to look alike.

Why would an antiracist oppose color-blind rhetoric and any attempts to make us all look alike?

"Across history, racist power has produced racist ideas about the racialized ethnic groups in its colonial sphere and ranked them— across the globe and within their own nations."

My ethnicity is African American, distinguishing me from Nigerians or Haitian Americans, even as we are all racialized as Black.

Rank three ethnic groups that are considered the most inferior within your race. Why are these ethnicities considered the most inferior? Why is it important for antiracists not to view these ethnicities as inferior?

1

2

3

_____

_____

_____

_____

_____

_____

_____

_____

_____

List five disparaging ideas about your racialized ethnic group. Share when you first heard or expressed them.

1

2

3

4

5

Why is it important for you not to believe these ideas about your racialized ethnic group or other ethnic groups within or outside your race?

"I believed that violence [defined] all the Black people around me, my school, my neighborhood. I believed it defined me—that I should fear all Darkness, up to and including my own Black body."

Describe a moment in your life when the
presence of an unknown Black or Brown body
scared you. Explain why you were so fearful
and why you should not have been so fearful.

_____

_____

_____

_____

_____

_____

_____

_____

_____

_____

_____

_____

_____

_____

_____

_____

_____

Many Black and Brown people do not like wearing hoodies or masks outside, even during pandemics, like the COVID-19 outbreak.

Why are Black and Brown people afraid of scaring others when they go outside?

Describe a time when you were in a familiar or an unfamiliar Black or Brown space and worried that something would happen to you—and nothing did happen to you. Was the space the problem or were your ideas about the space the problem? Explain.

Recall a recent racial injustice you witnessed. Racial profiling? Police violence? Racial slur? Did you say something or do something? Why or why not?

**Recall a recent racial injustice in society
that affected you—made you sad or angry or
prompted you to take action. Why did this
racial injustice affect you so deeply?**

Do you believe Black neighborhoods are dangerous? What makes you believe or disbelieve this idea?

_____

_____

_____

_____

_____

_____

_____

_____

_____

_____

_____

_____

_____

"The idea of the dangerous Black neighborhood is the most dangerous racist idea."

The harmful idea of the "dangerous Black neighborhood"

List two ways this dangerous idea affects housing policy, housing values, or housing decisions.

1 _____
_____

2 _____
_____

List two ways this dangerous idea affects educational policy, school values, or educational decisions.

1 _____
_____

2 _____
_____

List two ways this dangerous idea affects business policy, business values, or business decisions.

1 _____
_____

2 _____
_____

List two ways this dangerous idea affects policing policy, police fears, or policing decisions.

1 _____
_____

2 _____
_____

List two examples of when this dangerous idea affected your own decisions.

1 _____
_____

2 _____
_____

Upper-income Black neighborhoods have lower levels of violent crime than lower-income Black neighborhoods—as is the case among every race. Dangerous Black neighborhoods are actually dangerous *unemployed* neighborhoods.

What does this mean? What bearing would this more accurate framing have on anticrime policy?

How can we go about disconnecting Blackness from criminality?

"There is no such thing as a dangerous racial group. But there are, of course, dangerous individuals."

Why is it harmful to consider one racial group to be dangerous and other racial groups to be safe? How can that racist idea open us all up to personal harm?

Describe an instance in your life when you mistook someone as safe, due to their racial identity, and the person turned out to be dangerous or harmful.

For most of my life, I expressed both culturally antiracist and assimilationist ideas. I expressed Black cultural pride and I thought Black people should assimilate into White American culture.

Describe your cultural perspective(s). Consider your segregationist, assimilationist, and/or antiracist ideas.

"The Ave. I just loved being surrounded by all those Black people—or was it all that culture?—moving fast and slow, or just standing still. The Ave had an organic choir, that interplay of blasting tunes from the store to the car trunk, to the teen walking by practicing her rhymes, to the cipher of rappers on the corners. Gil would freestyle; I would listen and bob my head. The sound of hip-hop was all around us."

How would you define culture?

What constitutes an American to you?

Is America unicultural or multicultural? When you think of American culture, what religion, language, philosophy, art forms, food, and clothing do you think about? What American group practices these cultural ways of being? Should we be calling this "American" culture?

If you are an immigrant, share a moment
when you experienced xenophobia. If you are
not an immigrant, share a moment when you
participated in or witnessed xenophobia.

What are the negative effects of ascribing specific behaviors to specific racial groups?

"Racial-group behavior is a figment of the racist's imagination. Individual behaviors can shape the success of individuals. But policies determine the success of groups. And it is racist power that creates the policies that cause racial inequities."

Before you started on this journaling journey, what did you think were the racial behaviors of Black people?

What did you think were the racial behaviors of Asian people?

What did you think were the racial behaviors of Indigenous people?

What did you think were the racial behaviors of White people?

What did you think were the racial behaviors of Middle Eastern people?

What did you think were the racial behaviors of Latinx people?

DATE   /   /

What are the negative effects of all forms of bigotry?
What are the negative effects of ascribing specific
behaviors to specific gender groups? To transgender
people? To those in specific classes? To those
with specific sexual orientations? To those who
are disabled?

Describe a time when you did not treat an
individual as an individual or when you chalked
up someone's behavior to someone's race.

_____

_____

_____

_____

_____

_____

_____

_____

_____

_____

_____

_____

_____

_____

_____

_____

"An antiracist treats and remembers
individuals as individuals."

How should we disentangle identity, culture, behavior, and race?

What work needs to be done to treat people as *individuals*? Is that hard to do? Why?

Let's think about your upbringing. When was the first
time you remember skin color or hair texture being
addressed in your home, classroom, or community? What
was said? What lessons did you internalize?

"Colorism: A powerful collection of racist policies that lead to inequities between Light people and Dark people, supported by racist ideas about Light and Dark people. . . . Colorist ideas are also assimilationist ideas, encouraging assimilation into—or transformation into something close to—the White body."

Many people believe the lighter the skin color the better, the straighter the hair the better. What do you believe? What do you consider to be the human beauty standard?

I wore color contacts in college, thinking lighter eyes made me more handsome.

Have you ever transformed or thought about transforming your appearance to make yourself look like you're a different race or ethnicity?

_____

_____

_____

_____

_____

_____

_____

_____

_____

_____

_____

_____

_____

_____

_____

_____

_____

_____

_____

_____

In your institution or community, are darker people of color more likely to be in less desirable roles than lighter people of color and White people? Think about the color character of your environment.

_____

_____

_____

_____

_____

_____

_____

_____

_____

_____

_____

_____

"To be an antiracist is to focus on color lines as much as racial lines, knowing that color lines are especially harmful for Dark people."

What policies could be changed to create more equity in your institution or community between lighter people, darker people, and White people?

List three facts about your views on race that you must face about yourself.

1

2

3

List three forms of new knowledge you've gained about yourself through this racial journaling experience that you must accept.

1

2

3

"Malcolm X once said, 'I have always been a man who tries to face facts, and to accept the reality of life as new experience and new knowledge unfolds it.'"

Why is facing facts and accepting new knowledge essential to being antiracist?

_____

_____

_____

_____

_____

_____

_____

_____

_____

_____

_____

_____

_____

_____

_____

_____

_____

_____

_____

Why is refusing to face facts and rejecting new knowledge essential to being racist?

Not all White people benefit equally from racist policies affecting people of color.

What groups of White people benefit the most? What groups of White people benefit the least?

_____

_____

_____

_____

_____

_____

_____

_____

_____

_____

_____

_____

_____

_____

_____

"[R]acist power thrives on anti-White racist ideas—more hatred only makes their power greater."

How does our focus on White people as the problem—
instead of racist power and policy—lead to the
strengthening of racist power and policy?

"I learned . . . that every time I say something is wrong with Black people, I am simultaneously separating myself from them, essentially saying 'them niggers.' When I do this, I am being a racist."

Many people refuse to believe that one can be racist toward their own racial group.

Why do you think there is so much resistance to this idea?

Before reading the quote on the facing page, consider how you understand your own power.

Did your understanding of power make you feel powerless or powerful?

_____

_____

_____

_____

_____

_____

_____

_____

_____

_____

_____

_____

_____

_____

_____

_____

_____

_____

_____

"The powerless defense does not consider people at all levels of power, from policymakers like politicians and executives who have the power to institute and eliminate racist and antiracist policies, to policy managers like officers and middle managers empowered to execute or withhold racist and antiracist policies. Every single person actually has the power to protest racist and antiracist policies, to advance them, or, in some small way, to stall them."

Racist ideas make us feel powerless, and when we feel powerless, we don't resist.

Have you ever felt powerless? Share your story.

**How do you think
slaveholders tried to
make enslaved Africans
feel powerless?**

**How do you think Jim
Crow segregationists
tried to make Black
people feel powerless?**

How do you think
xenophobes today
are trying to make
Latinx immigrants
feel powerless?

How do you think
racist Americans
are trying to make
antiracist Americans
feel powerless?

Do you have policymaking power, policy-
managing power, and/or the power to resist
policy? Consider what kind of power you have.

DATE / /

List three new ways you can begin using your power in the racial struggle.

1

2

3

Name a racist idea you heard this month in your workplace, on the news, or in casual conversation that you wish you had responded to. Reflect on how you could have deployed your power differently in that moment.

A summary of my racial life:

"When we stop denying the duality of racist and antiracist, we can take an accurate accounting of the racial ideas and policies we support. For the better part of my life I held both racist and antiracist ideas, supported both racist and antiracist policies; I've been antiracist one moment, racist in many more moments."

_____

_____

_____

_____

_____

_____

_____

_____

_____

_____

_____

_____

_____

_____

_____

_____

_____

_____

Was the previous question hard to write about? How did responding to it make you feel?

Who is more of the problem—the person who refuses to acknowledge their racism or the person who admits their racism? Why?

_____

_____

_____

_____

_____

_____

_____

_____

_____

_____

_____

_____

_____

_____

_____

_____

_____

_____

Consider the ways in which class and race intersect in your neighborhood.

"Poor people are a class, Black people a race. Black poor people are a race-class."

What kind of ideas about poor people did the people who raised you have? How would you compare your ideas now to their ideas then?

DATE / /

I grew up thinking there was something wrong with practically every race-class, including my own group of middle-income African Americans.

What about you? Are there any beliefs about race-classes that stand out in your upbringing?

_____

_____

_____

_____

_____

_____

_____

_____

_____

_____

_____

_____

_____

_____

_____

_____

_____

_____

_____

_____

What policies,
historically or
currently, could be
behind the struggles
of impoverished
Indigenous people?

What policies,
historically or
currently, could be
behind the struggles of
the most impoverished
immigrant group in New
York City—Asians?

Black elites have less wealth than White elites. What policies, historically or currently, could be causing the wealth gap?

Describe some of the conditions in neighborhoods where poor Black people live that class antiracists should be focused on changing, instead of the people.

"To be antiracist is to equalize the race-classes. To be antiracist is to root the disparities between the equal race-classes in the policies of class racism. . . . To be antiracist is to say the political and economic conditions, not the people, in poor Black neighborhoods are pathological."

Poor Black people are said to live in the "ghetto" and be "ghetto" people. Poor White people are often labeled as "White trash." How are these examples of class racism?

What *privileges* do poor White people typically have when compared to poor Black people? What group is more likely to live in neighborhoods with higher concentrations of poor people? Why?

Americans struggle to define *capitalism* as they struggle to define *racism*. I find that people who love capitalism and those who loathe capitalism tend to define the term differently.

DATE   /   /

How do you define *capitalism*?

_____

_____

_____

_____

_____

_____

_____

_____

_____

_____

_____

_____

_____

_____

_____

_____

_____

_____

_____

**What do you see as the relationship between
capitalism and racism in your community?**

Make a list of the racialized spaces around you (including those that should be racialized as White). How do people commonly rank and view these spaces?

"Just as racist power racializes people, racist power racializes space. The ghetto. The inner city.

How are we hindering Black spaces when each time someone makes a mistake we blame the space or the institution, and not the individual?

"How many times did I individualize the error in White spaces, blaming the individual and not the White space? How many times did I generalize the error in the Black space—in the Black church or at a Black gathering— and blame the Black space instead of the individual?"

List five Black spaces or institutions that are routinely devalued and degraded.

1

2

3

4

5

Do these Black spaces or institutions have fewer resources than comparable White spaces or institutions? What policies could be behind these resource disparities? How can we go about eliminating the resource disparities between spaces?

_____

_____

_____

_____

_____

_____

_____

_____

_____

_____

_____

_____

_____

_____

_____

_____

_____

_____

Some people of color oppose eliminating the
spaces made and operated by people of color.
Why do you think that is so?

What kind of ideas about race did the people who raised you have? How would you compare your ideas now to their ideas then?

Segregationists want to eliminate Black people. Assimilationists want to eliminate the cultures of Black people.

Why do you think assimilationists identify so strongly as "not-racist"?

"Through lynching Black bodies, segregationists are, in the end, more harmful to Black *bodies* than integrationists are. Through lynching Black cultures, integrationists are, in the end, more harmful to *Black* bodies than segregationists are."

Segregationists aim to exploit Black spaces. Assimilationists aim to eliminate Black spaces.

DATE   /   /

Why have both been harmful to the livelihood of spaces where Black people predominate?

At Temple University during graduate school, Kaila and Yaba were two of my friends who were crucial in encouraging me to confront my bigotry. "I arrived at Temple as a racist, sexist homophobe. Not exactly friend material for these two women. But they saw the potential in me I did not see in myself."

Describe two people in your life who have been critical in putting up a mirror to your own bigotry.

What kind of ideas about one's sexual orientation did the people who raised you have when you were growing up? How would you compare your ideas now to their ideas then?

What kind of ideas about gender did the people who raised you have when you were growing up? How would you compare your ideas now to their ideas then?

"To truly be antiracist is to be feminist. To truly be feminist is to be antiracist."

Many people wrongly think feminists hate men.

Since feminists don't hate men, what or who do feminists really dislike? What are they fighting for?

_____

_____

_____

_____

_____

_____

_____

_____

_____

_____

_____

_____

_____

_____

_____

_____

_____

_____

_____

Like *racism* and *capitalism,* people have trouble defining *feminism.*

DATE   /   /

How do you define *feminism*? Once you've written your definition, search out a definition from a scholar of feminism. Compare your definition to, and contrast it with, the scholar's definition.

_____

_____

_____

_____

_____

_____

_____

_____

_____

_____

_____

_____

_____

_____

_____

_____

_____

Feminists of color have argued that White feminists too often consider elite White women to be the prototypical women.

Specify three cases of this.

1

2

3

Feminists of color have argued that some White feminists standardize the oppression faced by elite White women.

DATE   /   /

List three cases of this.

1

2

3

How is the oppression
faced by poor Indigenous
women the same as, and
different from, the
oppression faced by
elite White women?

How is the oppression
faced by elite Asian
women the same as, and
different from, the
oppression faced by
poor White women?

Feminists of color have argued that men of color too often consider themselves to be the representatives of their races.

Name three cases of this.

1

2

3

Feminists of color have argued that men of color too often standardize the oppression faced by men of color.

Specify three cases of this.

<u>1</u>

<u>2</u>

<u>3</u>

How is the oppression
faced by Black women the
same as, and different
from, the oppression
faced by Black men?

How is the oppression
faced by Latinx women the
same as, and different
from, the oppression
faced by Latinx men?

Can someone who primarily advocates for White women truly be feminist? Can someone who primarily advocates for men of color truly be antiracist? Why or why not?

I spent most of my life advocating for Black men and erroneously thought I was advocating for Black people. What race-gender(s) have you truly advocated for?

How do you define *homophobia*? How do you
define *transphobia*?

DATE   /   /

_____

_____

_____

_____

_____

_____

_____

_____

_____

_____

_____

_____

_____

_____

_____

"We cannot be antiracist if we are
homophobic or transphobic."

List five ways homophobia and transphobia intersect with racism to degrade and harm queer and trans people of color.

1

2

3

4

5

Black transgender women reportedly have the low-
est life expectancy among any racial group.

Why do you think that is the case?

_____

_____

_____

_____

_____

_____

_____

_____

_____

_____

_____

_____

_____

_____

_____

_____

_____

_____

Before starting on this racial journey, how did you view . . .

GAY BLACK MEN?

GAY MEN OF ANY RACE?

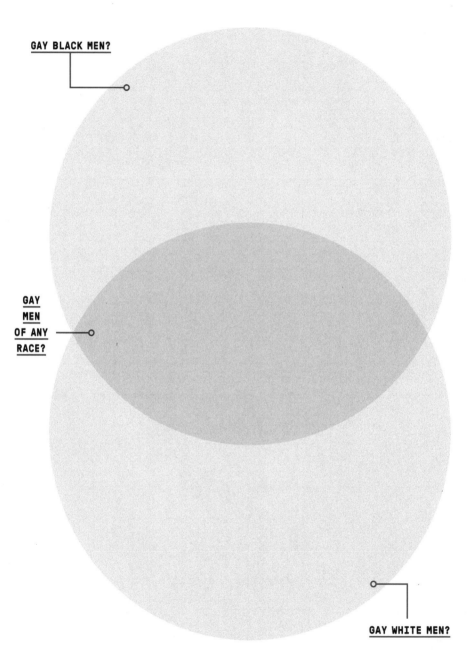

GAY WHITE MEN?

How did your views differ when it came to gay Black men as opposed to gay White men?

Consider the intersection of race, sexual orientation, and class. According to the Family Equality Council and Center for American Progress, "32 percent of children being raised by Black male same-sex couples live in poverty, compared to 14 percent of children being raised by White male same-sex couples, 13 percent of children raised by Black heterosexuals, and 7 percent of children raised by White heterosexuals."

What policies—or lack thereof—are behind these statistics?

How would you define *queer antiracism*?

"It is best to challenge ourselves by dragging ourselves before people who intimidate us with their brilliance and constructive criticism."

Kaila and Yaba, graduate school class-mates, were intimidating people for me.

Who are intimidating people for you?

How does racism breed cowardice?

"I am fearful of cowardice.
Cowardice is the inability to amass
the strength to do what is right in
the face of fear."

How does cowardice breed racism?

It took me many years to overcome my cowardice.

What about you? Where are you in the struggle against cowardice?

"Racial history does not repeat harmlessly. Instead, its devastation multiplies when generation after generation repeat the same failed strategies and solutions and ideologies, rather than burying past failures in the caskets of past generations."

Since the 18th century, racial reformers have been trying to educate away and love away racism.

DATE   /   /

List three strategies that have been used over the years that have largely failed to defeat or eliminate racist policies and ideas.

1

2

3

Why have these strategies continued to fail?

_____

_____

_____

_____

_____

_____

_____

What ideas about racism caused Americans to keep pursuing those failed strategies?

What is the source of racism?

What are your antiracist superpowers? How can
you regularly assist the individuals, campaigns,
policymakers, and organizations that are struggling
against racial inequity and racial injustice?

Who are your favorite antiracist leaders, writers, artists, or activists? Of your friends, family, and colleagues, whom do you admire most for their antiracist efforts? Why?

DATE   /   /

Of your close friends, family, and colleagues, whom do you loathe the most for their racism? Why? How has their racism affected your relationship?

Before helping someone you know to be antiracist, it is vitally important to take your time and strengthen the relationship by promoting mutual trust.

Why do you think this is so vital?

_____

_____

_____

_____

_____

_____

_____

_____

_____

_____

_____

_____

_____

_____

_____

_____

_____

_____

_____

As you strengthen the relationship, it is important to get to know your loved one really well, and get to know what is behind their racism. No one is born a racist.

What is your hypothesis right now about the roots of that individual's racism? Why is it vitally important to wholly understand these roots?

How can you contribute to an antiracist
future in your home, among your friends,
within your family, within your community?

Your home

Your friends

Your family

Your community

"Success. The dark road we fear. Where antiracist power and policy predominate. Where equal opportunities and thus outcomes exist between the equal groups. Where people blame policy, not people, for societal problems. Where nearly everyone has more than they have today."

Envision the world described on the facing page.

Describe what that world could look like and could be like. Why would nearly everyone have more in a world where antiracist power and policy predominate?

_____

_____

_____

_____

_____

_____

_____

_____

_____

_____

_____

_____

_____

_____

_____

_____

_____

_____

_____

"Our world is suffering from metastatic cancer. Stage 4. Racism has spread to nearly every part of the body politic."

As someone who had to fight metastatic cancer, it seems to me that the societal fight against racism is similar to the bodily fight against metastatic cancer. Let's break down this analogy by comparing terms of cancer and racism: If racism is a cancer, then surgery equates to removing racist policy; and implementing antiracist policies equates to the systemic treatment of chemotherapy that aims to shrink the tumors of inequity or prevent their reoccurrence.

What do you think about this analogy between fighting metastatic racism and metastatic cancer?

Being diagnosed with racism is not unlike being diagnosed with cancer. Both can be shocking and devastating. But people tend to respond to each of these very differently.

How? Why?

_____

_____

_____

_____

_____

_____

_____

_____

_____

_____

_____

_____

_____

_____

_____

_____

_____

_____

_____

_____

Why is pain essential to healing America of racism? Why is pain essential to healing ourselves of racism? Are you ready for the healing pain? Why or why not?

_____

_____

_____

_____

_____

_____

_____

_____

_____

_____

_____

_____

"When it comes to healing America of racism, we want to heal America without pain, but without pain, there is no progress."

To be antiracist is to be hopeful. We must all find hope.

How do you think you can find hope?

"The antiracist power within is the ability to view my own racism in the mirror of my past and present, view my own antiracism in the mirror of my future, view my own racial groups as equal to other racial groups, view the world of racial inequity as abnormal, view my own power to resist and overtake racist power and policy."

Look within. Describe your antiracist power.